The Crowd

is

Untruth

Søren Kierkegaard
(1813–1855)

The Crowd *is* Untruth

Søren Kierkegaard

On *the* Dedication *to*
"That Single Individual"[2]

Translated *by*
Charles K. Bellinger

---

[2] This, which is now considerably revised and enlarged, was written and intended to accompany the dedication to "that single individual," which is found in "*Upbuilding Discourses in Various Spirits.*" Copenhagen, Spring 1847.

"In a certain sense nothing can be spoken of so briefly as the Good, when it is well described. For the Good without condition and without qualification, without preface and without compromise, is absolutely the only thing that a man may and should will, and is only one thing. Oh blessed brevity, oh blessed simplicity, that seizes swiftly what cleverness, tired out in the service of vanity, may grasp but slowly! That which a simple soul, in the happy impulse of a pious heart, feels no need of understanding in an elaborate way, since he simply seizes the Good immediately, is grasped by the clever one only at the cost of much time and much grief."[1]

[1] *Upbuilding Discourses in Various Spirits*: "Purity of Heart is to Will One Thing" (1847) Søren Kierkegaard

The Crowd *is* Untruth

My dear, accept this dedication; it is given over, as it were, blindfolded, but therefore undisturbed by any consideration, in sincerity. Who you are, I know not; where you are, I know not; what your name is, I know not. Yet you are my hope, my joy, my pride, and my unknown honor.

It comforts me that the right occasion is now there for you; which I have honestly intended during my labor and in my labor. For if it were possible that reading what I write became worldly custom, or even to give oneself out as having read it, in the hope of thereby winning something in the world, that then would not be the right occasion, since, on the contrary, misunderstanding would have triumphed, and it would have also deceived me, if I had not striven to prevent such a thing from happening.

This, in part, is a possible change in me, something I even wish for, basically a mood of soul and mind, which does not produce change by being more than change and therefore produces nothing less than change; it is rather an admission, in part a thoroughly and well thought-out view of "life," of "the truth," and of "the way."

There is a view of life which holds that where the crowd is, the truth is also, that it is a need in truth itself, that it must have the crowd on its side.[3] There is another view of life; which holds that wherever the crowd is, there is untruth, so that, for a moment to carry the matter out to its farthest conclusion, even if every individual possessed the truth in private, yet if they came together into a crowd (so that "the crowd" received any decisive, voting, noisy, audible importance), untruth would at once be let in.[4]

For "the crowd" is untruth. Eternally, godly, christianly what Paul says is valid: "only one receives the prize," (I Cor. 9:24)[5] not by way of comparison, for in the comparison "the others" are still present. That is

---

[3] Perhaps, however, it is right to note once and for all, that which follows of itself and which I have never denied, that in relation to all temporal, earthly, worldly ends the crowd can have its validity, even its validity as a decisive court of last resort. But I am not speaking about such things, which I pay so little attention to. I speak of the ethical, the ethical-religious, of "the truth," and seen ethico-religiously the crowd is untruth, when it is taken as a valid court of last resort for what "the truth" is.

[4] Perhaps, however, it is right to note, although it seems to me to be almost superfluous, that it naturally could not occur to me to object to something, for example that there is preaching, or that "the truth" is proclaimed, even though it was to an assembly of a hundred thousand. No, but even if it were an assembly of just ten - and if there should be balloting, that is, if the assembly were the court of last resort, if the crowd were the decisive factor, then there is untruth.

[5] Know ye not that they that run in a race run all, but one receiveth the prize? Even so run; that ye may attain.

to say, everyone can be that one, with God's help – but only one receives the prize; again, that is to say, everyone should cautiously have dealings with "the others," and essentially only talk with God and with himself – for only one receives the prize; again, that is to say, the human being is in kinship with, or to be a human is to be in kinship with the divinity. The worldly, temporal, busy, socially-friendly person says this: "How unreasonable, that only one should receive the prize, it is far more probable that several combined receive the prize; and if we become many, then it becomes more certain and also easier for each individually." Certainly, it is far more probable; and it is also true in relation to all earthly and sensuous prizes; and it becomes the only truth, if it is allowed to rule, for this point of view abolishes both God and the eternal and "the human being's" kinship with the divinity; it abolishes it or changes it into a fable, and sets the modern (as a matter of fact, the old heathen) in its place, so that to be a human being is like being a specimen which belongs to a race gifted with reason, so that the race, the species, is higher than the individual, or so that there are only specimens, not individuals. But the eternal, which vaults high over the temporal, quiet as the night sky, and God in heaven, who from this exalted state of bliss, without becoming the least bit dizzy, looks out over these innumerable millions and knows each single individual; he, the great examiner, he says: only one receives the prize; that is to say, everyone can receive it, and everyone ought to become this by oneself, but only one receives the prize. Where the crowd is, therefore, or where a decisive importance is attached to the fact that there is a crowd, there no one is working, living, and striving for the highest end, but only for this or that earthly end; since the eternal, the decisive, can only be worked for where there is one; and to become this by oneself, which all can do, is to will to allow God to help you – "the crowd" is untruth.

A crowd – not this or that, one now living or long dead, a crowd of the lowly or of nobles, of rich or poor, etc., but in its very concept[6] is untruth, since a crowd either renders the single individual wholly unrepentant and irresponsible, or weakens his responsibility by making it a fraction of his decision. Observe, there was not a single soldier who dared lay a hand on Caius Marius; this was the truth. But given three or four women with the consciousness or idea of being a crowd, with a certain hope in the possibility that no one could definitely say who it was or who started it: then they had the courage for it; what untruth! The untruth is first that it is "the crowd," which does either what only the single individual in the crowd does, or in every case what each single individual does. For a crowd is an abstraction, which does not have hands; each single

---

[6] The reader will therefore recall, that here by "crowd," "the crowd" is understood as a purely formal conceptual definition, not what one otherwise understands by "the crowd," when it supposedly is also a qualification, when human selfishness irreligiously divides human beings into "the crowd" and the nobles, and so forth. God in heaven, how would the religious arrive at such in-human equality! No, "crowd" is the number, the numerical; a number of noblemen, millionaires, high dignitaries, *etc.* — as soon as the numerical is at work, the "crowd" is "the crowd."

individual, on the other hand, normally has two hands, and when he, as a single individual, lays his two hands on Caius Marius, then it is the two hands of this single individual, not after all his neighbor's, even less – the crowd's, which has no hands. In the next place, the untruth is that the crowd had "the courage" for it, since never at any time was even the most cowardly of all single individuals so cowardly, as the crowd always is. For every single individual who escapes into the crowd, and thus flees in cowardice from being a single individual (who either had the courage to lay his hand on Caius Marius, or the courage to admit that he did not have it), contributes his share of cowardice to "the cowardice," which is: the crowd. Take the highest, think of Christ – and the whole human race, all human beings, which were ever born and ever will be born; the situation is the single individual, as an individual, in solitary surroundings alone with him; as a single individual he walks up to him and spits on him: the human being has never been born and never will be, who would have the courage or the impudence for it; this is the truth. But since they remain in a crowd, they have the courage for it – what frightening untruth.

The crowd is untruth. There is therefore no one who has more contempt for what it is to be a human being than those who make it their profession to lead the crowd. Let someone, some individual human being, certainly, approach such a person, what does he care about him; that is much too small a thing; he proudly sends him away; there must be at least a hundred. And if there are thousands, then he bends before the crowd, he bows and scrapes; what untruth! No, when there is an individual human being, then one should express the truth by respecting what it is to be a human being; and if perhaps, as one cruelly says, it was a poor, needy human being, then especially should one invite him into the best room, and if one has several voices, he should use the kindest and friendliest; that is the truth. When on the other hand it was an assembly of thousands or more, and "the truth" became the object of balloting, then especially one should god-fearingly – if one prefers not to repeat in silence the Our Father: deliver us from evil – one should god-fearingly express, that a crowd, as the court of last resort, ethically and religiously, is the untruth, whereas it is eternally true, that everyone can be the one. This is the truth.

The crowd is untruth. Therefore was Christ crucified, because he, even though he addressed himself to all, would not have to do with the crowd, because he would not in any way let a crowd help him, because he in this respect absolutely pushed away, would not found a party, or allow balloting, but would be what he was, the truth, which relates itself to the single individual. And therefore everyone who in truth will serve the truth, is *eo ipso*[7] in some way or other a martyr; if it were possible that a human being in his mother's womb could make a decision to will to serve "the truth" in truth, so he also is *eo ipso* a martyr, however his martyrdom comes about, even while in his mother's womb. For to win a crowd is not so great a trick; one only needs some talent, a certain dose of untruth and a

---

[7] By that itself : by that fact alone -

little acquaintance with the human passions. But no witness for the truth – alas, and every human being, you and I, should be one – dares have dealings with a crowd. The witness for the truth – who naturally will have nothing to do with politics, and to the utmost of his ability is careful not to be confused with a politician – the god-fearing work of the witness to the truth is to have dealings with all, if possible, but always individually, to talk with each privately, on the streets and lanes – to split up the crowd, or to talk to it, not to form a crowd, but so that one or another individual might go home from the assembly and become a single individual. "A crowd," on the other hand, when it is treated as the court of last resort in relation to "the truth," its judgment as the judgment, is detested by the witness to the truth, more than a virtuous young woman detests the dance hall. And they who address the "crowd" as the court of last resort, he considers to be instruments of untruth. For to repeat: that which in politics and similar domains has its validity, sometimes wholly, sometimes in part, becomes untruth, when it is transferred to the intellectual, spiritual, and religious domains. And at the risk of a possibly exaggerated caution, I add just this: by "truth" I always understand "eternal truth." But politics and the like has nothing to do with "eternal truth." A politics, which in the real sense of "eternal truth" made a serious effort to bring "eternal truth" into real life, would in the same second show itself to be in the highest degree the most "impolitic" thing imaginable.

The crowd is untruth. And I could weep, in every case I can learn to long for the eternal, whenever I think about our age's misery, even compared with the ancient world's greatest misery, in that the daily press and anonymity make our age even more insane with help from "the public," which is really an abstraction, which makes a claim to be the court of last resort in relation to "the truth"; for assemblies which make this claim surely do not take place. That an anonymous person, with help from the press, day in and day out can speak however he pleases (even with respect to the intellectual, the ethical, the religious), things which he perhaps did not in the least have the courage to say personally in a particular situation; every time he opens up his gullet – one cannot call it a mouth – he can all at once address himself to thousands upon thousands; he can get ten thousand times ten thousand to repeat after him – and no one has to answer for it; in ancient times the relatively unrepentant crowd was the almighty, but now there is the absolutely unrepentant thing: No One, an anonymous person: the Author, an anonymous person: the Public, sometimes even anonymous subscribers, therefore: No One. No One! God in heaven, such states even call themselves Christian states. One cannot say that, again with the help of the press, "the truth" can overcome the lie and the error. O, you who say this, ask yourself: Do you dare to claim that human beings, in a crowd, are just as quick to reach for truth, which is not always palatable, as for untruth, which is always deliciously prepared, when in addition this must be combined with an admission that one has let oneself be deceived! Or do you dare to claim that "the truth" is just as quick to let itself be understood as is untruth, which requires no previous knowledge, no schooling, no discipline, no abstinence, no self-denial, no honest self-concern, no patient labor! No, "the truth," which detests this untruth, the only goal of which is to desire its increase, is not so quick on its feet. Firstly, it cannot work through the fantastical, which is the untruth; its communicator is only a single individual. And its communication relates itself once again to the single individual; for in this view of life the single individual is precisely the truth. The truth can neither be communicated nor be received without being as it were before the eyes of God, nor without God's help, nor without God being involved as the middle term, since he is the truth. It can therefore only be communicated by and received by "the single individual," which, for that matter, every single human being who lives could be: this is the determination of the truth in contrast to the abstract, the fantastical, impersonal, "the crowd" – "the public," which excludes God as the middle term (for the personal God cannot be the middle term in an impersonal relation), and also thereby the truth, for God is the truth and its middle term.

And to honor every individual human being, unconditionally every human being, that is the truth and fear of God and love of "the neighbor"; but ethico-religiously viewed, to recognize "the crowd" as the court of last resort in relation to "the truth," that is to deny God and cannot possibly be to love "the neighbor." And "the neighbor" is the absolutely true expression for human equality; if everyone in truth loved the neighbor as himself, then would perfect human equality be unconditionally attained; everyone who in truth loves the neighbor, expresses unconditional human equality; everyone who is really aware (even if he admits, like I, that his effort is weak and imperfect) that the task is to love the neighbor, he is also aware of what human equality is. But never have I read in the Holy Scriptures this command: You shall love the crowd; even less: You shall, ethico-religiously, recognize in the crowd the court of last resort in relation to "the truth." It is clear that to love the neighbor is self-denial, that to love the crowd or to act as if one loved it, to make it the court of last resort for "the truth," that is the way to truly gain power, the way to all sorts of temporal and worldly advantage – yet it is untruth; for the crowd is untruth.

But he who acknowledges this view, which is seldom presented (for it often happens, that a man believes that the crowd is in untruth, but when it, the crowd, merely accepts his opinion *en masse*, then everything is all right), he admits to himself that he is the weak and powerless one; how would a single individual be able to stand against the many, who have the power! And he could not then want to get the crowd on his side to carry through the view that the crowd, ethico-religiously, as the court of last resort, is untruth; that would be to mock himself. But although this view was from the first an admission of weakness and powerlessness, and since it seems therefore so uninviting, and is therefore heard so seldom: yet it has the good feature, that it is fair, that it offends no one, not a single one, that it does not distinguish between persons, not a single one. A crowd is indeed made up of single individuals; it must therefore be in everyone's power to become what he is, a single individual; no one is prevented from being a single individual, no one, unless he prevents himself by becoming many. To become a crowd, to gather a crowd around oneself, is on the contrary to distinguish life from life; even the most well-meaning one who talks about that, can easily offend a single individual. But it is the crowd which has power, influence, reputation, and domination – this is the distinction of life from life, which tyrannically overlooks the single individual as the weak and powerless one, in a temporal-worldly way overlooks the eternal truth: the single individual.

Note: The reader will recall, that this (the beginning of which is marked by the atmosphere of its moment, when I voluntarily exposed myself to the brutality of literary vulgarity) was originally written in 1846, although later revised and considerably enlarged. Existence, almighty as it is, has since that time shed light on the proposition that the crowd, seen ethico-religiously as the court of last resort, is untruth. Truly, I am well served by this; I am even helped by it to better understand myself, since I will now be understood in a completely different way than I was at the time, when my weak, lonely voice was heard as a ridiculous exaggeration, whereas it can now scarcely be heard at all on account of existence's loud voice, which says the same thing.

"If it is to be possible that a man can will only one thing then he must will the Good... To will only one thing: but will this not inevitably become a long drawn-out talk? If one should consider this matter properly must he not first consider, one by one, each goal in life that a man could conceivably set up for himself, mentioning separately all of the many things that a man might will? And not only this; since each of these considerations readily becomes too abstract in character, is he not obliged as the next step to attempt to will, one after the other, each of these goals in order to find out what is the single thing he is to will, if it is a matter of willing only one thing? Yes, if someone should begin in this fashion, then he would never come to an end. Or more accurately, how could he ever arrive at the end, since at the outset he took the wrong way and then continued to go on further and further along this false way? It is only by a painful route that this way leads to the Good, namely, when the wanderer turns around and goes back. For as the Good is only a single thing, so all ways lead to the Good, even the false ones — when the repentant one follows the same way back."[8]

---

[8] *Upbuilding Discourses in Various Spirits*: "Purity of Heart is to Will One Thing" (1847) Søren Kierkegaard

www.ingramcontent.com/pod-product-compliance
Lightning Source LLC
Chambersburg PA
CBHW030014040426
42337CB00012BA/779